The Future of TECHNOLOGY

What Is the Future of 3D Printing?

Hal Marcovitz

ReferencePoint Press®

San Diego, CA

© 2017 ReferencePoint Press, Inc.
Printed in the United States

For more information, contact:
ReferencePoint Press, Inc.
PO Box 27779
San Diego, CA 92198
www.ReferencePointPress.com

LIBRARY OF CONGRESS CATALOGING-IN-PUBLICATION DATA

Names: Marcovitz, Hal, author.
Title: What is the future of 3D printing?/by Hal Marcovitz.
Description: San Diego, CA: ReferencePoint Press, Inc., [2017] | Series: What Is the Future of
    Technology? | Audience: Grades 9-12. | Includes bibliographical references and index.
Identifiers: LCCN 2015046402 (print) | LCCN 2015048445 (ebook) | ISBN 9781682820667
    (hardback) | ISBN 9781682820674 (epub)
Subjects: LCSH: Three-dimensional printing--Juvenile literature. | Technological innovations--
    Juvenile literature.
Classification: LCC TS171.95 .M385 2017 (print) | LCC TS171.95 (ebook) | DDC 621.9/88--dc23

LC record available at http://lccn.loc.gov/2015046402

Contents

Important Events in the Development of 3D Printing

1968
French engineer Pierre Bezier creates Unisurf, the first CAD program that enables designers to model in 3D.

1986
In March Hull establishes 3D Systems in Rock Hill, South Carolina, to manufacture 3D printers for industrial uses. In October Carl Deckard, a graduate student at the University of Texas, develops the second 3D printing process: selective laser sintering.

2006
Italian engineer Enrico Dini develops the first D-Shape printer, to be used in the construction of homes and other buildings.

1960 1970 1980 1990 2000

1983
California engineer Chuck Hull invents the first 3D printing process, stereolithography.

2002
Researchers at Wake Forest University School of Medicine in North Carolina design a 3D printer capable of using human cells as the additive, specifically to create a human kidney.

1962
The first widely used computer-aided design program is developed by Ivan Sutherland at the Massachusetts Institute of Technology.

1988
The third 3D printing process, fused deposition modeling, is created by Scott Crump, an engineer from Minnesota.

2015
In January the British biotechnology company Open Bionics unveils an inexpensive 3D-printed prosthetic hand that employs electromyography, which enables the brain to control the movement of the prosthetic; in October a group of eight architects wins an award from the National Aeronautics and Space Administration for designing Ice House, a concept for a 3D-printed habitat on Mars.

2007
Local Motors, which proposes to make automobiles through 3D printing, is established in Phoenix, Arizona.

2010
Kor Ecologic of Winnipeg, Canada, prints the Urbee, a prototype for a car capable of driving cross-country on 10 gallons (37.8 L) of gasoline.

2012
The Belgian 3D printing company LayerWise uses titanium as the additive to create a lower jaw for a patient whose jaw was afflicted by disease.

2005   **2010**   **2015**

2009
Bre Pettis, Zach Smith, and Adam Mayer found MakerBot Industries in New York City and a short time later develop the first 3D printers marketed to consumers.

2013
The e-NABLE network, a group of CAD modelers who volunteer to make 3D-printed prosthetic limbs for patients, is founded by Jon Schull, a research scientist at the Rochester Institute of Technology.

2011
A joint project by engineers at the universities of Exeter and Brunel in Great Britain modify an ink-jet printer to print candies using chocolate as the additive.

2014
In April the WinSun Decoration Design Engineering Company of China prints the components for ten homes and erects the homes within a few hours; in December astronauts aboard the International Space Station use a 3D printer to make a wrench—the first object created in space through additive manufacturing.

Introduction

The Potential of 3D Printing

From Theory to Application

3D printing enables users to create tangible objects employing a device connected to a computer, similar to how a standard printer creates documents or photographs. Objects are created by feeding an additive such as plastic, metal, or glass into the printer. The additive is first heated into molten, or liquid, form. It is then laid down on the printer bed by a nozzle that follows a design created on the computer using 3D modeling software. Although 3D printing was first developed in the 1980s, its application has largely been confined to industrial purposes. In recent years, though, designers have found ways to make consumer products on 3D printers, opening a wide horizon of applications for the technology. Moreover, desktop 3D printers have been developed for hobbyists, enabling people to create their own projects through the technology.

Most people buy clothes the same basic way: They select a few jackets, dresses, or pairs of pants off the store racks, then retreat into tiny fitting rooms to see how they look. After wearing the clothes for no more than a few minutes and eyeing themselves in the fitting room mirrors, they make decisions on which garments to buy. Sometimes they get the fit right, but sometimes they do not.

The way people buy clothes may change dramatically in the

future. Not only would shoppers be guaranteed precise fits in their garments, they would also have the option of adding personalized touches to their clothing: patterns they design themselves, insignias or names of favorite bands, or their own initials on their collars or T-shirts. Even those who lack skills with needle and thread may be able to make their own clothes. Says *Vogue* magazine fashion writer Robert Sullivan, "How close are we to that scenario becoming reality? Well, we have the tools."[1]

The technology that may change the way people fill their closets in the future is 3D printing. For years the technology has been applied mostly to industrial uses, such as making gears, levers, and other components for machinery. In the past decade, though, desktop 3D printers have been developed for consumer use. And as the technology continues to evolve, many entrepreneurs, engineers, and designers are looking at the potential of 3D printing and finding

WORDS IN CONTEXT

entrepreneur
An individual who seeks to grow a business using innovative concepts, such as applying new technology to consumer goods.

that the process could lead society in exciting new directions, revolutionizing manufacturing, medicine, transportation, and architecture. Says Christopher Barnatt, a professor of computer science at Nottingham University in Great Britain, "Within a decade or so, it is likely that a fair proportion of our new possessions will be printed on demand in a local factory, in a retail outlet, or on a personal 3D printer in our own homes. . . . While the required technology to allow this to happen is still in its infancy, 3D printing is developing very rapidly indeed."[2]

Length, Width, and Height

Just as a conventional printer produces documents, a 3D printer produces objects in three dimensions: length, width, and height. And although many different substances—including plastics, glass, metals, and ceramics—can be used to compose the objects, the one substance that cannot be fed into a 3D printer is fabric. 3D printers work by heating the substances that are fed into them to high temperatures. Glass, for example, has to be heated to a temperature of 2,900°F (1,600°C) for it to be melted and made into a pliable substance by a 3D printer. Heating fabrics like cotton or wool to such high temperatures would obviously destroy them.

And yet 3D printing has the capability to make clothes, because clothes made on 3D printers are not made out of fabrics. Instead, fashion designers have found they can print very thin layers of plastics that possess the look and feel of fabric. Moreover, by using scanning technology, which can provide a 3D digital image as well as the dimensions of a customer's body, a designer can tailor a garment specifically to the size and shape of the customer—thereby guaranteeing a good fit. Says Dutch fashion designer Iris van Herpen, who is now designing many of her creations for 3D printing, "I'm really happy that 3D prints finally act with the movement of the body. Now a girl can even dance in it. [My] last show was really a big step forward because it [included clothes that were] totally flexible and the jacket we created, for example, you could put in the washing machine. You could sit on it. It's really a garment now."[3]

A Future Filled with 3D Printing

Although designers like Van Herpen are starting to incorporate 3D-printed outfits into their selections, other fashion experts wonder whether 3D-printed clothes will turn out to be popular among customers. Says Sophia Amoruso, chief executive officer of fashion retailer Nasty Gal, "To me it feels really unnatural, inhuman. It takes the fun out of shopping. I don't want to drag and drop my outfit onto myself."[4] The question of whether 3D printing will come to dominate the fashion industry probably will not be answered for many years, since many designers and retailers slowly test customers' tastes before they make full commitments to the technology. Therefore, it is likely that at least for the near future, most clothes will continue to be made of fabric in factories.

A woman examines a garment that Dutch fashion designer Iris van Herpen created using 3D printing technology. Articles of clothing made with this method are constructed of thin layers of plastic rather than cloth.

Still, there is no question the technology of 3D printing will continue to advance. Says Barnatt:

> Some people may tell you that 3D printing is currently being overhyped and will have little impact on industrial practices and our personal lives. Yet these are the same kinds of individuals who once told us that the Internet was no more than a flash in the pan, that online shopping would have no impact on traditional retail, and that very few people would ever carry a phone in their pockets.[5]

If 3D printing holds that type of potential, then years from now people who wear 3D-printed clothes, drive 3D printed cars, and live in 3D-printed houses may wonder what life would be like without their 3D printers.

Chapter 1

What Is 3D Printing?

3D printing is a process that creates an object using a device connected to a computer. The device, known as a 3D printer, is similar to the conventional printer that produces paper versions of text documents, photographs, and other illustrations. Unlike a conventional printer, though, the 3D printer "prints" in three dimensions, creating a tangible object that can be held in the hand or even driven on a highway, sailed on a river, or used as a home.

Although 3D printing was first developed in the 1980s, until recently it was largely reserved for industrial applications. Manufacturers have employed 3D printers to make tiny parts installed in machines or used the process to custom-make products for clients. Among corporations a common use for the technology is to make prototypes—objects that are made as part of a test phase—before using conventional manufacturing to mass-produce the objects. Companies can use the 3D printing process to make prototypes cheaply for testing purposes before they commit large sums of money to manufacturing the objects by the hundreds of thousands or even millions.

WORDS IN CONTEXT

prototype
An early version of a product made during a test phase.

The cost of 3D printers can vary widely. Typically, a 3D printer employed for industrial purposes is large and expensive, costing hundreds of thousands of dollars. In 2009 engineers for MakerBot Industries of New York City developed the first 3D printers marketed to consumers. Printers sold to consumers can sit on desktops next to home computers. Many consumer 3D printers cost less than $1,000.

The Maker Community

Since the introduction of 3D printers for consumers, a community of "makers" has grown as hobbyists use the technology to fashion objects for their homes. For example, by using their 3D printers, hobbyists can print their own custom Christmas ornaments featuring images of their children. Golfers can print their own golf tees, imprinting their names along the sides of the tees. Chess players can print their own customized chess pieces. Musicians can print their own electric guitars, adding personalized features such as images of themselves or their favorite rock stars. People can print their own smartphone cases, including their names and colorful designs on the covers.

Joshua Pearce, a professor of engineering at Michigan Technological University in Houghton, Michigan, serves as an example of a typical maker. He regularly strolls through the aisles of stores such as Walmart, scanning the shelves in search of inspiration for projects he can make on his 3D printer at home. He says, "I take great pleasure—and my wife teases me about it—walking through Walmart and saying, 'I could print that, I could print that, I could print that.'"[6]

Indeed, the potential of 3D printing is restricted only by the talents, skills, and imaginations of the makers. Says Christopher Barnatt, "Never in history have the opportunities been so great for so many people to start designing and manufacturing things in new ways."[7]

Subtractive Manufacturing

Prior to the introduction of 3D printing, manufacturing had largely been regarded as a "subtractive" process. This means that in conventional manufacturing the finished product is made from raw materials that are, essentially, subtracted from the process as the product moves down an assembly line. In fact, manufacturing has been regarded as subtractive since the era of the Industrial Revolution, dating back more than two centuries.

Workers pour molten metal into molds from which finished products will emerge when the metal cools and hardens. This kind of manufacturing process is known as subtractive *because the material from which the product is made is gradually subtracted from the original quantity as the item moves through the production process.*

Typically, manufacturers mass-produce products in one of two ways: They either make them from molds or die cut them from raw materials. To make a kitchen saucepan, for example, a manufacturer may create a mold of a saucepan using a ceramic material. The metal used for the saucepan will be heated to a high temperature so that it melts. The molten metal is then poured into the mold, where it cools and hardens. The finished pan is removed from the mold, which is then used again to make another saucepan. Of course, in a busy factory there are numerous molds being filled at the same time.

Another manufacturer may produce saucepans through the die-cutting process. First, a metal die is fashioned in the shape of the saucepan. The die is then fixed to a press. Next, huge sheets of metal are fed into the press. The die slams down on the metal sheet, cutting the saucepan out of the raw material. As with the mold process, a factory may employ numerous die-cutting presses, all working nonstop to create saucepans that will be sold in stores.

Both processes are subtractive. After the saucepans are made, there is leftover material: unused molten metal or scraps from the sheet metal used in the die-cutting process. And although the leftover material is often recycled and fed back into the manufacturing process, a lot of the waste material is tossed out. According to the US Department of Energy, the amount of waste generated by subtractive manufacturing is significant. Says the agency, "Many conventional manufacturing processes—which have recently been termed 'subtractive manufacturing'—require cutting away excess materials to make the desired part. The result: Subtractive manufacturing can waste up to 30 pounds of material for every 1 pound of useful material in some parts."[8]

Layer by Layer

In contrast to the old-style method of subtractive manufacturing, 3D printing is regarded as "additive" manufacturing. The additive is the material fed into the 3D printer that is used to create the object. The additive can be made of all manner of substances. For hobbyists, the additive is typically a thin string of pliable plastic held by a spool in the back of the machine. Industrial users may use pulverized or molten metal, glass, ceramics, or concrete. Food can even be used as an additive—bakers have used chocolate to 3D print customized candies.

A conventional printer uses ink to create a document or photograph. In one common printing process, known as ink-jet printing, the ink sprays out of a nozzle that slides back and forth above the page. The nozzle is controlled by the computer, which commands the printer to produce a document or image to re-create, on paper, the text or image that appears on the computer screen. 3D printing employs

WORDS IN CONTEXT

subtractive
The manufacturing process in which raw material, such as metal or wood, is removed—or subtracted—from the product.

WORDS IN
CONTEXT

additive
A substance such as
plastic or glass that
is fed into the 3D
printer to produce
the object.

a very similar process. The additive—whether it is plastic, concrete, or chocolate—is fed into a nozzle that follows the design of the object. The printer applies the additive layer by layer, slowly building the object from bottom to top.

Additive manufacturing produces no waste. All additive fed into the device is used to manufacture the object through the 3D printing process. That is why 3D printing can be a substantially cheaper process than subtractive manufacturing—the company needs to obtain smaller quantities of raw materials to make the same number of products. Moreover, 3D printing is regarded as far more environmentally friendly than conventional manufacturing; since all the additive is used in the manufacturing process, none of it ends up in landfills or incinerators.

Stereolithography

Although all 3D printing requires the use of an additive to make an object, there are three separate methods that have been developed to apply the additive to the project. The first method developed to print objects in 3D is known as stereolithography. The process was developed in 1983 by engineer Chuck Hull of Valencia, California. In stereolithography the additive is heated and liquefied before it enters the nozzle. The additive then hardens as it emerges from the nozzle. The term owes its name to the artistic process known as lithography, which dates back to the eighteenth century. To create a lithograph, ink is applied to a flat, moist sheet of paper that has been treated with grease. The greased area of the paper absorbs the ink, but the moist and ungreased areas of the paper do not. Through this process, the lithographic image emerges. Therefore, the nozzle of the 3D printer builds upon the surface by applying layers of additive, much as a lithographer applies layers of ink.

Hull invented stereolithography as a method of speeding up the process to make prototypes of parts used in industrial applications. At the time, prototypes often had to be handmade by craftspeople—known in industry as model makers—in their shops. It was a process that could take six weeks or more. "And when you got the prototype it was usually wrong," Hull says. "But you couldn't start [using it] and improving until you got it."[9]

At the time, Hull worked for a company that applied laminate—a thin layer of plastic—to tabletops. The laminate is applied as a coating to the tabletop, protecting the surface from damage caused by bumps or dings. The laminate is applied in liquid form, hardening as it emerges from a nozzle. Hull concluded that he could apply a second layer atop the original layer of laminate, followed by another layer on top of the second, and so on. And through this process, he could create a tangible object—to his thinking, the prototype of a gear, socket, or similar part used in industrial machinery. He says, "I saw those coatings as thin pieces of plastic and I thought that if I could stack those up to make a solid shape, it might be a way of solving the prototyping problem."[10] The first object Hull created through stereolithography was a tiny cup.

Useful Ideas or Junk?

Thingiverse is a popular Internet site where makers can find projects to download and print on their home 3D printers. The site is sponsored by MakerBot Industries, a New York City–based manufacturer of consumer 3D printers. By 2015 makers had uploaded designs for more than five hundred thousand projects on the site.

Although Thingiverse has the potential to help spark an interest in 3D printing among potential makers, critics argue that sites like Thingiverse do little more than enable people to make useless household goods that will eventually be thrown away. After visiting Thingiverse, technology writer Rachel Ehrenberg said she found designs for homemade projects such as models of the Eiffel Tower, a plastic octopus wearing a top hat and monocle, and various heart-shaped bracelet charms. "Junk proliferates on Thingiverse," she concluded. Added Joshua Pearce, a dedicated maker and a professor of engineering at Michigan Technological University in Houghton, Michigan, "There is a lot of stuff that has no value, no improvement for humanity. There is a possible moral hazard that we will make more junk."

Rachel Ehrenberg, "The 3D Printing Revolution," *Science News*, March 9, 2013, p. 20.

Inside a Typical Desktop 3D Printer

Industrial-sized 3D printers are still more common than desktop 3D printers, but the latter have significantly improved over the last decade. The typical desktop device prints objects using a corn-based renewable plastic or other synthetic material **(1)**. To print objects, a robotic print head and extruder **(2)** operate like a hot-glue gun—layering the plastic on a build plate **(3)** that moves down as each layer of the object is printed. Using local controls **(4)**, the maker sets print settings that determine the object's size and other characteristics.

Desktop 3D printers rely on a printing method known as fused deposition modeling, or FDM. To print an object using this method, the print head first makes an outline of the object on the surface of the build plate **(A)**. The outlined shape is then filled in with a cross-hatch pattern **(B)**. The build plate moves downwards as new layers are outlined and filled **(C)**, eventually resulting in the completed object.

Source: *Wall Street Journal*, "MakerBot Replicator Mini Review: 3-D Printing Comes Home," June 17, 2014, www.wsj.com.

Toy Frog

A second method of 3D printing is known as selective laser sintering (SLS). The process was developed in 1986 by Carl Deckard, a computer science graduate student at the University of Texas. In SLS the additives are applied in powdered form, then heated and compacted—or "sintered"—into a solid mass by a laser beam. As with stereolithography, the additive is applied through a nozzle. Also, the nozzle as well as the laser beam are guided on their paths by the computer to follow the design.

The final method of 3D printing is known as fused deposition modeling (FDM). The process was developed in 1988 by Scott Crump, an engineer from Eden Prairie, Minnesota. The project that launched FDM technology was a toy frog, which Crump attempted to fashion for his young daughter by using a hobbyist's glue gun that he loaded with candle wax and liquid polyethylene (a plastic used to make grocery bags.) After laboring to make the frog, layer by layer, by using the glue gun, Crump envisioned a way to automate the process. He recalls thinking, "What if I could take an ink pen and output plastic? What if I could do it with metal?"[11]

FDM is the process employed in consumer 3D printers, with the additive fed into the nozzle in a thin, spaghetti-like strand of plastic that is held on a spool behind the printer. The strand, known as filament, is heated by the printer as it enters the nozzle and emerges from the nozzle in molten form, making it soft and flexible. Essentially, the printer fuses the filament, also known as the deposit, into the object.

Computer-Aided Design

Whether the 3D printer sits on a factory floor or the desktop of a maker, the object produced by the printer must first be designed. In the precomputer age, designing a saucepan, Christmas ornament, automobile, home, or skyscraper was performed at a drafting table. Professional designers employed tools such as rulers, T squares, triangles, French curves, protractors, and mechanical pencils to create designs on paper. These designs were often referred to as "blueprints" because the drawings were rendered in white lines against blue backgrounds.

3D Selfies

Selfies are a common part of popular culture. Thanks to 3D printing, 3D selfies—known as shapies—may find a place in popular culture as well.

The Palo Alto, California, company Artec Industries has established scanning booths in shopping malls and theme parks. Digital scanning dates back to the 1970s: The technology creates images of documents and photographs. The page to be scanned is laid facedown on a flatbed scanner, which uses a technology known as optical character recognition to capture the image and transfer it to a computer. Artec's Shapify booths employ scanners housed on panels that revolve around the person standing inside. Afterward, the scan is transferred to a computer and printed on a 3D printer.

In 2015 technology writer Eddie Krassenstein and his wife, Whitney, stood inside a Shapify booth at the Freehold Raceway Mall in Freehold, New Jersey. Wrote Krassenstein:

> I had the chance to pose with Whitney as the massive machine made a full 360-degree rotation around us in just twelve seconds. Using four wide-view, high resolution scanners, the machine was able to capture us from virtually every angle possible. . . . I was very impressed by the detail that it captured. Everything from my wife's wedding ring to intricate wrinkles in my khaki pants were captured perfectly.

Eddie Krassenstein, "Artec 3D Brings Incredible Shapify Booths to New Jersey Mall & I Got to Try One Out," 3DPrint.com, April 8, 2015. http://3DPrint.com.

Computer keyboards have long since replaced drafting tables, T squares, and blueprints. As far back as 1962, the first computer-aided design (CAD) programs were developed, enabling designers to sketch projects on computer screens rather than on drafting tables. In fact, one of the first widely used CAD programs—developed by Ivan Sutherland, a professor at the Massachusetts Institute of Technology—was known as Sketchpad.

Sketchpad and the other early CAD programs enabled designers to make use of their computers, but these programs still rendered designs in two dimensions. A breakthrough occurred in 1968 when Pierre Bezier, an engineer employed by the French automaker Renault, designed Unisurf, the first program that enabled designers to model projects in three dimensions. Because 3D printing would not be developed for another fifteen years, Unisurf and the other early 3D CAD programs could not be applied to the direct manufacture of objects, although they still served as important tools for designers.

As the technology of 3D printing emerged, programmers were able to adapt 3D modeling software as drivers for the printers. 3D CAD programs that are commonly used today include Rhinoceros by software designer Robert McNeel & Associates of Seattle, Washington, and SolidWorks by Dassault Systèmes of Waltham, Massachusetts. Finally, the Mill Valley, California, software designer Autodesk has produced two CAD programs, AutoCAD and Inventor.

Years of Training

These programs are known as solid modeling or hard modeling programs, which are used for product design. This means that by creating their designs using Rhinoceros or one of the other programs, designers can render the object on the screen, then view any side or angle on the screen merely by entering commands that will flip or spin the virtual object. Finally, when the design has been completed, the user essentially presses the Print command, and the 3D printer produces the object.

Many amateurs have acquired CAD skills that enable them to design objects like smartphone cases or golf tees on their desktop 3D printers. In addition, many websites have been established that enable amateurs to upload their designs and make them available to anyone who wishes to download the designs and print their own projects. Therefore, many owners of 3D printers may not possess CAD skills at all but simply use their devices to print projects that have been designed by others.

Although many amateurs can make objects with their 3D printers with limited or even no knowledge of CAD, designing objects in three dimensions is performed at its highest level by professionals, known as CAD modelers or 3D designers. Typically, CAD modelers are graduates of university art or engineering programs.

Computer-assisted design (CAD) programs enable users to model designs for products in three dimensions and rotate them for viewing from any angle. Here, an object created using this kind of software and 3D printing is displayed next to the original design for it.

Because of the complexity of the CAD software, it could take years for CAD modelers to master the programs that have been written specifically for 3D design.

A Technology in Its Infancy

Although 3D printing was first developed in the 1980s, many experts agree that the era of 3D printing is still in its infancy. Unlike earlier generations, chances are the current generation of young people will be exposed to 3D printing before they reach adulthood, because many schools have purchased the devices and are providing students with opportunities to design and print their own projects. Says MakerBot founder Bre Pettis, "The students who get these printers start seeing the physical world differently, they start designing stuff, they're activated as entrepreneurs, they start making and selling, say, iPhone cases with the school's logo on them—and it all takes off from there."[12]

Therefore, in the future, it is likely that many people will possess CAD skills and be very comfortable with the notion that 3D printing can give them an alternative to products that are manufactured conventionally. Mark Fleming, founder of the website 3DPrinter.net, which follows developments in the 3D printing industry, says:

> 3D printing destroys the inefficient, 20th century manufacturing model and replaces it with a new paradigm that brings a reduction in design-to-manufacturing time, virtually eliminates storage and transportation costs, reduces resource consumption, allows us to make things that were not possible before, and democratizes the materialization of ideas so literally everyone can create. 3D printing will do to manufacturing what the Internet has done to communication.[13]

Around the globe, engineers, CAD modelers, and other professionals are envisioning new and exciting applications for 3D printing. In the future many experts believe 3D printing will do more than just create customized Christmas ornaments, golf tees, or gears and sockets hidden deep within complicated machines. It is expected that 3D printing will play a role in revolutionizing transportation, architecture, medicine, and even space travel.

Chapter 2

Opening a New Frontier in Transportation

Henry Ford revolutionized modern manufacturing in 1913 when he conceived of the assembly line to manufacture automobiles at his factory in Detroit, Michigan. Seventeen years earlier, however, Ford built his first automobile in his garage, piecing together the vehicle one part at a time over a period of many months. He sold the car for $200 and used the money to buy parts to make another car. Eventually, he started his own car company and, after revolutionizing mass production by installing an assembly line at his plant, became the top automaker in the world, churning out some 267,000 cars per year by 1914.

In the years since Ford revolutionized mass production, all other automakers have adopted his assembly-line techniques. Millions of new cars are produced each year by automakers based in America, Germany, Italy, Japan, South Korea, and other industrialized nations. Virtually all cars are made on assembly lines in what is regarded as a highly subtractive industrial process.

3D printing has the potential to change how cars—and other modes of transportation, including boats and airplanes—are made. Already, some small companies have made prototypes of cars produced through the 3D printing process. Moreover, some visionaries predict that in the future, the 3D printers available to consumers will have the capability to produce projects as large as cars. Says James Derek Sapienza, a New York City journalist who reports on the auto industry, "Imagine a day when the intrepid tinkerer can download, print, and build a car in his or her own garage. It may sound like science fiction, but it's coming sooner than you think."[14] Therefore, in the future it may be possible for the owner of a 3D printer to produce a car in his or her own garage—in the same spirit as Ford when he built his first car in his garage more than a century ago.

Restoring Classic Cars

The era when people can print their own cars in their garages is still very much in the future, given that most 3D printers available to consumers are desktop models. Therefore, at this point, the only car a consumer is capable of making under the current 3D technology is a toy-sized model car.

Using 3D Printing in the War on Poaching

Although airliner designers such as Bastian Schaefer of Airbus believe it would take an enormously large 3D printer to produce an aircraft through additive manufacturing, some 3D-printing advocates believe it may be possible to use currently available technology to produce smaller aircraft. One project under way to make 3D aircraft in the same fashion as boats and cars is being pursued by Toby Lankford, a farmer and environmental activist from Amarillo, Texas. Lankford has designed a 3D-printed drone aircraft that he hopes to employ over the skies of Africa to monitor the activities of poachers who kill endangered species and other protected animals. Known as the Icarus 3.0, the drone has a wingspan of about 6 feet (1.8m).

As with a car or boat produced on a 3D printer, the drone aircraft would not be made in one continuous printing operation. Rather, sections of the drone would be printed, then pieced together to create the aircraft.

Lankford believes the 3D-printed drone could be an effective weapon in the war on poaching. He says:

Poaching is an issue that presented itself as the most urgent. We are at extreme risk of driving [rhinoceroses] and elephants into extinction in this decade. There are fewer than 5,000 black rhinos left in the wild. They are being poached at a rate of over 1,000 per year. Elephants are losing their lives for their ivory at over 30,000 per year. It is a problem seeking an immediate solution.

Quoted in 3ders.org, "Texan Toby Lankford Designs 3D Printed, Solar Powered RC Drone as Anti-Poaching Tool," July 15, 2015. www.3ders.org.

But the existing technology suits Jay Leno, the comedian and former *Tonight Show* host, who owns an impressive collection of classic automobiles. Leno takes a personal hand in restoring the cars in his collection. And since the parts he may need to restore cars that were manufactured as long ago as Henry Ford's era are no longer widely available, Leno has found that 3D printing technology helps meet his needs. Using his desktop 3D printer, Leno is able to make his own replacement parts for the cars in his collection. "Let's say you have an older Cadillac or a Packard, and you can't get one of those beautifully ornate door handles," says Leno. "You could go to [a] big swap meet . . . every day for the rest of your life and never find it. Or you could take the one on the left side of your car, copy it, use the computer to reverse it, and put that new part on the other side."[15]

Leno's method of printing individual components to restore automobiles has been embraced by others, including many entrepreneurs who have established companies to 3D print entire cars. These entrepreneurs do not envision an entire automobile printed, bottom to top, in a single, continuous 3D printing session. Rather, they find it more realistic to print sections of a car, then piece those sections together to create a vehicle.

WORDS IN CONTEXT

hybrid
An automobile equipped with both an electric motor and an internal combustion engine; the car runs most of the time on the electric motor, with the gasoline-powered engine employed when battery power is low.

The Urbee 2

One of the companies that is exploring the manufacture of cars through 3D printing is Kor Ecologic, founded by mechanical engineer Jim Kor. The company, based in Winnipeg, Canada, is working to develop a 3D-printed car known as the Urbee 2. (The original Urbee is a prototype created by Kor that lacks an interior.) The Urbee 2 will operate on three wheels, carry a driver and one passenger, and be manufactured through the 3D printing process. To design the Urbee 2, CAD modelers have combined the thousands of parts found in the typical automobile into a few dozen segments.

The Urbee, an automobile produced entirely through 3D printing, is displayed at a show in Paris. Unlike many other objects that emerge from the 3D-printed process in whole form, the Urbee is printed in sections that are then put together to create the finished car.

After those segments are printed, they will be assembled into the Urbee 2. "The thesis we're following is to take small parts from a big car and make them single large pieces,"[16] says Kor.

The car is designed as a hybrid, meaning it would be powered mostly by an electric motor, but a gasoline-fueled internal combustion engine would also be installed in the event the batteries run down. Neither the electric motor nor the gasoline-powered engine would be 3D printed, but most other components of the car would be produced through additive manufacturing. Kor plans to make most of the car out of plastic, using the FDM process.

By using plastic as the additive, the car will be lighter than a typical conventionally manufactured vehicle, which is made mostly out of steel. Therefore, the Urbee 2 would be better able to save energy. A lighter car means the electric motor would not have to work as hard, which means the batteries remain charged longer.

Likewise, when the car does have to rely on the internal combustion engine for power, the Urbee 2's light weight means the engine could keep the car running on less fuel. The Urbee 2 will weigh about 1,200 pounds (544 kg). In contrast, the typical compact car manufactured on an assembly line weighs about 4,000 pounds (1,814 kg.) To demonstrate the fuel efficiency of the car, Kor hopes to take the Urbee 2 on a journey from San Francisco to New York City—a distance of 2,905 miles (4,675 km)—using just 10 gallons (38 L) of gasoline. By 2016 no date had been set for the cross-country test—the company was still attempting to raise funds to finance production of the first Urbee 2.

Open Source

Like Kor Ecologic, Local Motors of Phoenix, Arizona, hopes to produce automobiles through the 3D printing process, combining thousands of small parts into a few dozen printable sections. Unlike Kor, though, Local Motors has proposed to "open source" its designs.

Under the open source concept, a manufacturer makes the design available on the Internet and invites interested people to download the plans, improve on the design, and then send the design back to Local Motors. This concept is contrary to how manufacturing has been pursued for generations. Typically, companies guard their designs very closely, fearing that competitors would steal and therefore profit from their designs.

Officials at Local Motors believe, however, that a technology as cutting-edge as producing a car through 3D printing would be enhanced through the participation of people outside the company. "I've got the machines. You've got the brains," says Jay Rogers, chief executive officer of Local Motors, in explaining his company's dedication to open source design. "Let's bring the chocolate and the peanut butter together and let's make better cars."[17]

WORDS IN CONTEXT

open source
A manufacturing concept in which people who do not work for a company are invited to download the organization's plans for a product and suggest modifications.

By the time of this writing Local Motors had printed proto-types of a compact car, which it has named the Strati. As Local Motors moves forward, it intends to establish microfactories, small manufacturing establishments where 3D printers produce its automobiles. The first such microfactory is planned for Prince George's County in Maryland. At the microfactories, buyers would be invited to sit down with CAD modelers to help design the cars, bringing the individual touches they desire to the final designs. By giving buyers the opportunity to work with CAD model-

ers, people would not be making their own cars, but they would be able to participate in designing the vehicles—a concept that would take people a step closer to the day when they could create their own cars in their own garages.

Making Boats on 3D Printers

Although people cannot yet print their own cars at home, some people have been able to print another mode of transportation—their own seaworthy boats. Boat-racing enthusiast Walter Hole-mans, an aerospace engineer from Silver Spring, Maryland, was prompted to turn to 3D printing when he noticed the convention-ally manufactured rudder on his racing catamaran was increasing the drag on the boat, slowing it down.

Drag is the force that acts against a moving object, impeding its speed. In airplanes, drag is caused by air, which causes friction on the fuselage, wings, and tail. At sea, drag is caused by the force of water pressure against the hull as well as the rudder. The rudder is the component of the boat that rides underwater beneath the vessel. The rudder responds to the motion of the tiller, which the pilot uses to steer the boat.

A catamaran is an extremely light, double-hulled vessel that is ideal for racing. Powered by the wind, a catamaran skims along the top of the water at speeds of 34 miles per hour (55 kph) or more. The conventionally manufactured rudder on Holemans's vessel was made of wood, which featured a grainy surface.

Employing 3D printing, aerospace engineer Walter Holemans built a half-size version of a catamaran, a kind of lightweight sailing vessel. Here, full-sized catamarans skim across the water, powered by the wind.

Holemans found that the grainy surface increased the drag on the rudder, reducing the speed of the vessel.

So Holemans designed his own rudder, made of plastic. He initially planned to fashion a mold for the rudder, making the device by pouring molten plastic into the mold. He says, "I realized I could print the mold and then thought, 'Well, I could just print the rudder. I could print parts that would be impossible to machine.'"[18] So Holemans 3D printed the rudder, but then he took his project a step further. He designed a new miniature version of a catamaran and then printed the entire 8-foot (2.4-m) vessel, albeit in parts, which he then pieced together. The boat produced on Holemans's 3D printer is about half the size of a typical catamaran.

Robotboat

Holemans has been working to adapt the same technology to another project: producing robotically controlled 3D-printed boats that do not require human crews. The boats would not be raced but rather dispatched to remote regions for scientific and reconnaissance missions. For example, the boats could accumulate data on oil spills and other environmental hazards by employing scientific instruments that measure water temperature, wind speed, and water quality. The 3D-printed vessel could also search for plane wrecks or scout the open seas for illegal activity, such as smugglers or pirates. (Piracy off the west coast of Africa is a major concern to commercial mariners, whose ships have been seized by marauding bandits traveling in small speedboats.)

Holemans's company, Planetary Systems Corporation, has developed a prototype for the vessel, which he named Robotboat.

Making Bicycles Through 3D Printing

Bicycles are perhaps the most environmentally friendly mode of transportation in existence. Bicycles do not burn gasoline or other fossil fuels, which means they do not contribute to air pollution or global warming. However, most bicycles are still manufactured through a subtractive process—the steel frames are milled and fashioned through heavy industrial processes often fueled by coal- or gas-burning plants.

The production of bicycles may become much more environmentally friendly in the future if bicycle manufacturers adopt the techniques of EuroCompositi, a Padua, Italy, design firm. In 2015 EuroCompositi introduced the Bhulk, a mountain bike featuring a frame produced through FDM. Moreover, the additive used to make the Bhulk is polylactic acid, which is made from plants—mostly corn and sugarcane. In fact, the plants used to make the Bhulk frame were collected from waste gathered at food processing companies.

So not only is the Bhulk bike frame made out of green materials, it is made specifically of recycled green materials. Reported the website 3ders.org, "The . . . Bhulk could start a new trend. It's the first mountain bike where a 3D printer is used to make the frame from . . . recyclable and recycled materials."

Also, once the bike frame is no longer usable, it can be ground up and used for fertilizer—meaning it would not contribute to pollution in a landfill or incinerator. At the time of this writing EuroCompositi has given no timetable for when the company expects to bring the bicycle into production.

3ders.org, "EuroCompositi's 3D Printed PLA Bike Frame—Made from Plants—Wins Eurobike Gold Award," September 1, 2015. www.3ders.org.

Holemans suggests the Robotboat can reduce costs and keep people out of harm's way because it is small and needs no crew. Says T.J. Edwards, an engineer who worked on the prototype, "It has been a phenomenally helpful experience if one sees the boat as a remote sensor in a harsh environment that needs to be very robust. Robotboat has a lot of the same characteristics as satellites."[19]

Other projects to manufacture boats through the 3D printing process have ranged from kayaks that can be produced on consumer desktop printers to luxury yachts that will be marketed to wealthy boating enthusiasts. In 2014, for example, Livrea Yacht Italia, based in Modena, Italy, unveiled the Livrea26, a 26-foot (8-m) wind-powered yacht produced through SLS. As with projects such as the Urbee 2 and the Local Motors automobiles, the Livrea26 was not produced in a single continuous 3D printing session but rather pieced together from printed segments.

Meanwhile, in 2014 Charlotte, North Carolina, boating enthusiast Jim Smith used his desktop 3D printer to produce a kayak that measures 16 feet (5 m) in length and 2 feet (61 cm) in width. Smith works as an engineer for 3D Systems, a manufacturer of 3D printers that was founded by Chuck Hull. Smith printed the kayak in twenty-eight sections, then pieced them together using screws as well as caulk to ensure the seams are watertight. It took Smith forty-two days to print and assemble the kayak. Says Smith, "I really wanted to print something that would demonstrate the potential of 3D printing and customization for an individual. I had always enjoyed kayaking and since I live on a lake, a custom kayak would work perfectly."[20]

Making an Aircraft

Unlike the projects to produce operational cars and boats on 3D printers, no effort is believed to be under way to produce an entire aircraft through additive manufacturing. The main roadblock to 3D printing an entire aircraft is the lack of a printer large enough to undertake the job. As with the automobile- and boat-printing projects, the device would be designed to print just the components of the plane, rather than the entire plane in one

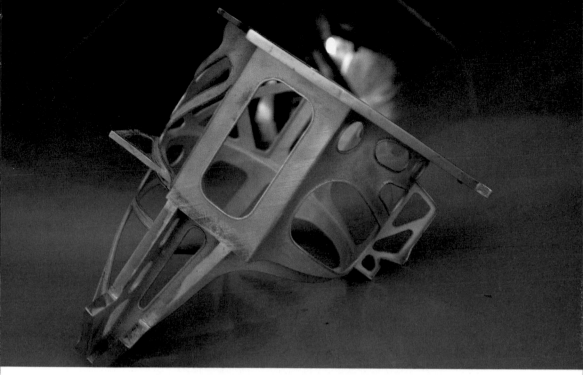

Because of their large size, airplanes are presumed not to be good candidates for production using 3D printing. Nonetheless, as with cars and boats, airplanes could potentially be constructed from individual 3D-printed components like the one pictured here, which is part of the landing gear.

continuous session. Nevertheless, Bastian Schaefer, an engineer with Airbus, the European commercial airline manufacturer, estimates that for his company's purposes, the project would require development of a printer that measures some 262 feet (80 m) in length—nearly the size of a football field. Still, Schaefer is optimistic that the project could eventually be tackled. "This could be feasible,"[21] he says.

In the meantime, aircraft manufacturers, using technology currently available, are making use of additive manufacturing. They employ the technology to make prototypes of aircraft components, or they 3D print various parts that are used in otherwise conventionally manufactured planes. Aircraft manufacturers have found that 3D-printed parts are lighter than parts machined through subtractive manufacturing. Lighter parts mean an overall lighter aircraft, which requires less fuel—an important consideration in aviation because a lighter plane could travel longer distances before needing to land at an airport for refueling. Says Eric Masanet, a professor of mechanical engineering at Northwestern University near Chicago, "There are enough parts that, when replaced, could reduce the weight of the aircraft by 4 to 7 percent. And it could be even more as we move forward. This will save a lot of resources and a lot of fuel."[22] In 2015 aircraft manufacturer GE Aviation announced that by 2020 it plans to make more than one hundred thousand different aircraft parts through additive manufacturing.

As the production of airplanes, boats, and automobiles moves into the future, it is clear that 3D printing will be an integral part of the transportation industry. Moreover, as the efforts of home-based makers such as Jim Smith illustrate, it is already possible to use 3D printers to make simple forms of transportation—such as a kayak—on a desktop printer. As printers for home use become more sophisticated in the future, it could be possible, as James Derek Sapienza suggests, for people to produce their own cars in their own garages. These amateur makers will be able to leave their own thumbprints on a transportation industry in transition, just as Henry Ford did more than a century ago.

Chapter 3

Revolutionizing Medicine Through 3D Printing

Each day, seventy-nine Americans receive organ transplants. These patients are often afflicted with diseases that cause their organs to fail. The most common cases involve transplants of kidneys, livers, hearts, and lungs.

Patients can obtain kidneys from living donors—everybody has two, and medical research had proved people can live full and healthy lives with a single kidney. Also, a patient can receive a portion of a liver from a living donor. The donated portion will grow into a complete organ. But in all other cases, the only way for a patient to receive an organ is from a person who has agreed to donate organs when he or she dies. Indeed, immediately after a donor's death the body is rushed to an operating room, where a surgeon "harvests" the fresh organs from the deceased person so that they may be transplanted into the bodies of patients who need them.

Many people willingly agree to donate their organs; nevertheless, there are not enough donors to meet the needs of people with failing kidneys and other organs. Indeed, many people are forced to spend months on waiting lists for organ donations, and very often their bodies succumb to disease before donor organs can be found. According to the US Department of Health and Human Services, about twenty-two people die every day because donor organs could not be found in time to save their lives.

Many medical researchers believe that in the future, there will be no waiting lists for organ transplants. In fact, there would no longer be a need to find people willing to donate their organs. 3D printing has the potential to make new organs for people, using human cells as the additive through a process known as bioprinting.

Undifferentiated Cells

Researchers have already taken the first steps toward creating human organs on 3D printers by successfully printing cells that knit together, forming very small pieces of human tissue. By 2015 tissue samples produced through 3D printing were no larger than a drop of water. In the future, though, researchers believe they will be able to design and print new hearts, lungs, kidneys, and other organs on 3D printers, then transplant those organs into patients by using common surgical techniques. "That's the ultimate goal of 3D bio-printing," says Jennifer Lewis, who leads a bioprinting research project at Harvard University in Cambridge, Massachusetts. "We are many years away from achieving this goal."[23]

The additives used in bioprinting are embryonic stem cells. Embryonic stem cells are formed in a very early stage of human development. This stage is known as the blastocyst, which contains between 150 and 200 human cells. The blastocyst forms about five days after the female egg has been fertilized by the male sperm. The blastocyst is no larger than a grain of sand. During the blastocyst stage, the cells are undifferentiated, meaning they have not yet turned into specific cells, such as skin cells, blood cells, or brain cells. The undifferentiated cells have the potential to form into cells that have these and other specific purposes.

After the cells are withdrawn from the donor, they are fed nutrients and nurtured in laboratory dishes so that they create stem cell lines, which contain millions of cells. Under experimental stem cell therapy, the undifferentiated stem cells are withdrawn from the line and injected into a patient's body, becoming specific cells that many researchers believe can replace cells afflicted with cancer and other diseases. Stem cell therapy has remained in the experimental phase since the 1960s; nevertheless, many physicians believe the therapy holds great promise to eradicate various diseases.

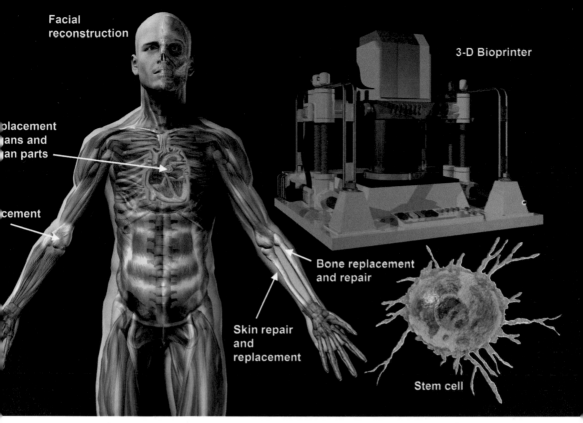

Facial reconstruction

3-D Bioprinter

placement
ans and
an parts

cement

Bone replacement
and repair

Skin repair
and
replacement

Stem cell

Although 3D printing of human tissue is in its infancy, many scientists believe that in the future, this technology will be capable of producing replacement organs and tissue for implantation into the human body. This chart shows possible uses for this technique, which is known as bioprinting.

Printing New Skin

As stem cells undergo experimental trials, the potential for using stem cells as an additive in 3D printing has attracted a lot of attention in the medical community. "Basically what it allows you to do is build tissue the way you assemble something with Legos," says Keith Murphy, chief executive officer of Organovo, a San Diego, California, company that is pursuing bioprinting. "So you can put the right cells in the right places. You can't just pour them into a mold."[24] Using the techniques of bioprinting, Organovo hopes to use 3D printing to make new human kidneys and lungs as well as bones, cartilage, muscle, and blood vessels.

One method of bioprinting under study does not require stem cells as an additive but rather can make use of the patient's own cells. This method of bioprinting seeks to create new skin on a 3D printer. The ability to produce new skin would prove to be a major medical breakthrough, particularly for burn victims.

Instead of relying on stem cells, physicians can use the existing healthy cells from the skin of the patients, then nurture them into reproducing themselves in a lab dish. When enough cells are available, they are fed into a 3D printer. "It's cutting edge," says Dr. Marc Jeschke, the director of Ross Tilley Burn Centre in Toronto, Canada, who developed a 3D printing process using skin cells. "We can mimic how your skin looks. And that's the evolvement, that's something new, that's something novel. . . . We grow these cells in various containers and make them exactly into the cell type that we want. [Then] the printer tells the cells where to go."[25] The skin that emerges from the nozzle of the printer is then grafted onto the patient through a surgical process.

By 2016 the process was still in the trial phase. However, Jeschke suggests that within a few years, 3D printers could become

A 3D-Printed Ear That Hears

Researchers at Princeton University in New Jersey used 3D printing in 2014 to fashion a prosthetic human ear that can enable a recipient to hear. To illustrate that such prosthetics can easily be fashioned, the researchers created the ear using a low-priced 3D printer marketed to amateur makers.

The additive for the printer consisted of cells drawn from calves as well as silver and other metals, which act as conductors of electrical current. After printing the ear, researchers inserted a coiled antenna consisting of two wires that detect sounds. The audible signals are transferred to the patient's nerve endings, similar to the way in which an ordinary hearing aid functions.

Says Michael McAlpine, a professor of mechanical and aerospace engineering at Princeton who headed the project, "The conventional microelectronics industry is really good at making 2D electronic gadgets. With TVs and phones, the screen is flat. But what 3D printing gives you is a third dimension, and that could be used for things that people haven't imagined yet, like 3D structures that could be used in the body."

Quoted in Heidi Milkert, "Princeton Researchers Create First Ever Completely 3D-Printed Quantum Dot LEDs," 3DPrint.com, November 5, 2014. http://3DPrint.com.

common devices in hospital burn units. In addition, since the 3D printer under development for the process is the size of a desktop printer, Jeschke sees a use for the device by military physicians. Soldiers are often burned during combat. Conceivably, Jeschke says, a field hospital equipped with a 3D printer could manufacture new skin for the burned soldier within minutes of the soldier arriving at the hospital, saving the soldier from a lifetime of disfigurement.

Printing Prosthetic Limbs

Using actual human cells to make new skin and organs such as kidneys, hearts, and lungs is still very much in the future. However, medical researchers have already made great strides in using 3D printers to make prosthetics—artificial versions of arms, hands, feet, and legs for people who have lost limbs due to accidents, diseases, or birth defects.

Prosthetic limbs typically cost between $10,000 and $80,000. A prosthetic limb must be designed to fit each patient, then individually manufactured. The prosthetic limb contains many moving parts that enable the patient to use the prosthetic much the same way he or she would use a hand or foot. For young people in need of prosthetics, the cost can be much greater because the young patient grows out of the prosthetic every few years, meaning a new mechanical limb must be designed and fitted to the patient. And, of course, the patient's family must shoulder the burden of paying for the new mechanical limbs.

But CAD modelers have found they can design new prosthetics for patients that can be 3D printed quickly and cheaply, oftentimes for no more than a few dollars. Indeed, in 2013 Jon Schull, a research scientist at the Rochester Institute of Technology in New York State, founded the e-NABLE network, a worldwide organization of CAD modelers who volunteer their time to design prosthetic limbs for patients. By 2015 e-NABLE had printed more

Four-year-old Briton Abbi Jillian displays her prosthetic hand. Replacement limbs like hers that are produced with 3D printing are much more durable and far less costly than traditional prosthetic limbs.

than fifteen hundred prosthetic limbs, charging patients no more than fifty dollars for the devices. Typically, the limbs are engineered so the devices respond to muscle movements. For example, the patient fitted with a prosthetic hand is able to use the fingers to grip an object by flexing muscles in the wrist.

Jorge Zuniga, director of the 3D Research & Innovation Laboratory at Creighton University in Omaha, Nebraska, says student CAD modelers at his school have participated in the e-NABLE project. He says, "Economic resources play a crucial role in prescription of prostheses for children, especially when private insurance and public funding are insufficient. Advancements in 3D printing offer the possibility of manufacturing . . . prosthetic devices at very low cost. The development of low-cost prosthetic devices is having a significant clinical and social impact on children around the world."[26]

One young patient who received a new 3D-printed prosthetic hand is Anastasia Rivas, a ten-year-old from North Bergen, New Jersey, who was born without a left hand. The prosthesis was made for her by Ty Esham, a CAD modeler from Decatur, Georgia, who produced the hand on his desktop 3D printer. Says Esham, "If she outgrows it, we can print another. If she breaks it, it's easy to fix. There are no batteries to recharge. She can get her hand wet and dirty; you can't do that with the expensive prosthetic hands, even though getting wet and dirty is what hands do! 3D printing gives you something lightweight, cheap, and functional."[27] As for Anastasia, she has found her new 3D-printed hand very user-friendly. "The kids at school think my [prosthesis] is really cool," says Anastasia. "Now I can pick up my eyeglass case, and I can pick up a pencil, although that is still hard to do—I keep practicing."[28]

Monitoring Signals from the Brain

Groups like e-NABLE have made great progress in establishing 3D printing as a viable alternative to the old-style practice of engineering prosthetic limbs, but so far the organization has reached relatively few patients. In the United States it is estimated that four out of ten thousand babies are born without limbs. Thousands more patients—both children and adults—lose limbs each year to diseases or accidents. Therefore, for 3D printing to make a difference in their lives, it would take much more than an organization of volunteer CAD modelers. Private companies in the medical industry must embrace 3D printing as a viable method for manufacturing prosthetic limbs, making them widely available as well as inexpensive for the patients.

One of the first companies to embrace the new technology is the Great Britain–based Open Bionics, which in 2015 announced that it had developed a 3D-printed prosthetic hand that would cost patients no more than $1,500. The prosthetic designed by Open Bionics is considered much more advanced than the mechanical limbs produced through the e-NABLE project. The Open Bionics prosthetic employs a procedure known as electromyography—a process for monitoring signals from the brain that control muscle movement.

The prosthetic limbs produced by Open Bionics include electronic sensors implanted into the muscles in the wrist that read the electromyographic signals, transferring them to the prosthetic. This process enables the patient to use all five fingers in the prosthetic as though they are made of flesh and bone. Joel Gibbard, a robotics engineer who developed the electromyographic prosthetic for Open Bionics, says, "We've encountered many challenges in designing our hands but the reactions of the individuals we help fuels our perseverance to bring them to market. My aim is for Open Bionics to disrupt the prosthetics industry by offering affordable prosthetics for all."[29]

The One-Size-Fits-All System

Using 3D printing technology to make new human organs or prosthetic limbs would have an impact on the lives of thousands of patients. Meanwhile, research is under way that would employ 3D printing for medical purposes that could potentially impact the lives of tens of millions of people.

Each day, millions of Americans consume prescription drugs—most often in pill form. Drugs are prescribed for a wide variety of ills. Among the pills consumed each day are painkillers for people who suffer from chronic pain, drugs that induce sleep for people who suffer from chronic insomnia, drugs that help widen blood vessels for people who suffer from high blood pressure, drugs that eliminate infections that cause illnesses, and drugs that help people combat depression and other mental illnesses. A 2013 study by the Minnesota-based Mayo Clinic estimated that seven out of ten Americans—or some 220 million people—consume prescription drugs. Twenty percent of Americans who consume prescription drugs take as many as five separate prescriptions.

Prescription drugs are manufactured by pharmaceutical companies, which typically make pills the same way that most consumer products are manufactured. The ingredients for the pills are fed into machines that formulate the ingredients into the drugs, transforming the concoctions into pill form—often stamping them out by the millions. The main drawback to the system is that pills cannot be made to suit the particular needs of individual patients. Pills are stamped out by the machines in common doses: 25 milligrams, 50 milligrams, 100 milligrams, and so on.

Although the one-size-fits-all system works for a lot of people, it falls short of the needs of many others. For some patients a 50-milligram dose of a particular prescription drug is not sufficient, but a 100-milligram dose is too much. Since the drug company

Walking Again in a 3D-Printed Exoskeleton

In 1992 Amanda Boxtel of Basalt, Colorado, was paralyzed in a skiing accident, which left her confined to a wheelchair. Twenty-two years later, she walked again, thanks to a motorized exoskeleton that was 3D printed.

CAD modelers working for Ekso Bionics of Richmond, California, scanned Boxtel's body, then designed a plastic exoskeleton, known as the Ekso-Suit, that fits snugly over the woman's torso and legs. Tiny yet powerful motors were installed in the exoskeleton, providing power for the legs to take strides. Electronic sensors that are connected to the muscles of Boxtel's spine and thighs send signals to the motors, activating them when she wishes to take steps. "After years of dreaming about it, I am deeply grateful and thrilled to be making history by walking tall in the first ever 3D-printed Ekso-Suit, made specifically for me," Boxtel said shortly after taking her first steps in more than two decades. "This project represents the triumph of human creativity and technology that converged to restore my authentic functionality in a stunningly beautiful, fashionable and organic design."

Quoted in Todd Halterman, "Amanda Boxtel Uses a 3D-Printed Exoskeleton to Defy Paralysis," 3D Printer World, February 19, 2014. www.3dprinterworld.com.

does not make a dose tailored specifically for the patient, the patient's doctor has no choice but to prescribe what is available, even though the doses that are available may not meet the patient's needs. Among the patients most affected by the current method of manufacturing prescription drugs are children. Young patients often have no choice but to take drugs that have been manufactured for adults, even though the doses may be much too strong for their bodies to absorb. As such, many young patients suffer from side effects, such as drowsiness or skin rashes, that are caused by the heavy doses of drugs.

3D Printing Prescription Drugs

Many medical researchers believe that in a few years, 3D printing will change the way doctors prescribe drugs as well as the way pharmaceutical companies supply medications. By using 3D printers, pharmaceutical companies can make prescriptions that fall between their mass-produced doses, printing individual pills that have been specifically prescribed for individual patients. The additives fed into the printer are the ingredients—the chemicals— that make up the drugs. Says Mohamed Albed Alhnan, a professor of pharmacy at the University of Central Lancashire in Great Britain, "At the moment we are making standard medicines, a one size fits all, but now the trend is to prescribe medicine specifically tailored for individual patients, which is where the new method comes in."[30]

Alhnan predicts that eventually, people may be able to make their own prescription drugs at home on their desktop 3D printers. For many patients, their symptoms fluctuate from time to time. When their symptoms are not severe, they may be able to live on smaller doses of their drugs. When symptoms flare up, though, they must contact their doctors and ask for new prescriptions featuring stronger doses of their drugs.

Alhnan suggests that if patients are supplied the raw materials for their drugs, they can respond to flare-ups of their symptoms on their own, printing their pills in doses that best control their symptoms. (A patient would still need to contact a doctor before printing his or her own pills. Most likely, the patient would send

Technicians mass-produce a prescription drug. Traditional manufacturing methods for these drugs result in medications in uniform dosages. By contrast, 3D printing may lead to doctors being able to prescribe a dosage individually tailored for a specific patient.

an e-mail to the doctor describing his or her symptoms, and the doctor would respond by providing the patient's 3D printer with the formula to tailor the dose to the patient's symptoms.) Says Al-hnan, "Eventually, we hope to see that units can be kept at home for patients who continuously need to change their daily dose."[31]

Improving People's Lives

In 2015 the US Food and Drug Administration (FDA), the agency that monitors all prescription medications sold in America, took a major step toward making 3D-printed pharmaceuticals a routine method of delivering medical care when it gave its approval for the first 3D-printed drug: Spritam, a drug prescribed for people who suffer from epilepsy. The drug, manufactured by Aprecia Pharmaceuticals of Langhorne, Pennsylvania, helps prevent epileptic patients from experiencing seizures.

The FDA has recognized that many people's lives can be affected if they are administered doses of their medications tailored specifically for their individual needs. In the future it is likely that many people's lives can be saved if organ donor waiting lists are eliminated through the adoption of bioprinting. And as medical device companies like Open Bionics embrace 3D printing, many people's lives can be improved if they can obtain prosthetic limbs quickly and inexpensively. As the research into 3D printing organs, prosthetics, and prescription drugs illustrates, additive manufacturing has the capability to dramatically change how medical care is delivered in America and elsewhere.

Chapter 4

From the Ground Up: Printing New Homes

The 3D printer built by WinSun Decoration Design Engineering, a construction company in China, is like few other printers on earth. The printer is composed of steel girders forming a rectangle. It stands 20 feet (6 m) high, 33 feet (10 m) wide, and 132 feet (40 m) long. The device weighs 120 tons (109 metric tons.) The nozzle rides below a steel girder powered by a huge motor that guides it as it lays down an additive made of recycled construction waste, such as old glass, ground steel, and cement. In 2014 the printer produced ten small homes as well as a five-story apartment building and an 11,840-square-foot (1,100-sq-m) mansion.

The printer did not create entire houses, bottom to top, on-site. Rather, the printer, located at the company's headquarters in the city of Shanghai, made components of the buildings—such as the walls, floors, doors, and windows. Those components were then trucked to the construction site and assembled into the completed structures. The whole process took far less time than the traditional stick-built method of erecting a home. (The term *stick-built* stems from the fact that in constructing a home, the structure rises from the foundation as carpenters erect lumber joists and studs—the sticks—that support the floors, walls, and ceilings.) Using construction techniques that have changed little over the centuries, carpenters, roofers, plumbers, electricians, masons, and other tradespeople ordinarily take weeks if not months to erect a single home.

> **WORDS IN CONTEXT**
>
> **joists**
> Horizontal support beams found in nearly all construction.

In contrast, in April 2014 WinSun erected all ten houses within twenty-four hours. And whereas the cost of even the smallest stick-built home could run $100,000 or more, WinSun listed the cost of its 3D-printed houses at $4,800 each. As for the mansion, a similar stick-built luxury home would ordinarily cost millions of dollars. WinSun said the cost of the mansion produced by its 3D printer is $161,000. Says Enrico Dini, an Italian civil engineer and head of Monolite UK, a London-based company also exploring 3D printing for construction purposes, "It would be very difficult to fabricate such large sections with traditional [construction methods]. With 3D printing, you have a lot less waste because you're only printing out as much material as you need and you can custom shape whole sections on the spot, which can be a big challenge."[32]

Recycling Waste

Monolite UK and WinSun are among a growing list of construction companies and architectural firms that see a bright future in 3D printing as an alternative to traditional stick-built construction. "I think [3D printing] is as fundamental a shift as the elevator was in raising our cities," says New York City architect Adam Kushner. "Let's forget about the act of construction being this difficult, time-consuming, energy-consuming part of our lives. We can build these amazing, beautiful structures and then let's do other things—let's go out there and enjoy the world around us."[33]

Cost—as evidenced by the prices charged by WinSun—is a major reason companies predict high demand for 3D-printed homes as well as other buildings. Ma Yihe, the head of WinSun and the designer of its 3D printer, says a significant factor in the low cost of 3D-printed homes is that the additive can be obtained for a fraction of the cost of traditional construction materials. Such materials include lumber, which is produced by chopping down trees and milling the wood into sticks and boards; concrete, which is composed of stone that must be mined or quarried; and steel,

A man visits one of ten 3D-printed houses built in Shanghai, China. Remarkably, all ten houses were erected within a twenty-four-hour period.

which is produced through a heavy industrial process that turns iron ore into construction-grade steel. "To obtain natural stone, we have to employ miners, dig up blocks of stone and saw them into pieces. This badly damages the environment," says Ma. "But with the 3D printing, we recycle mine [waste] into usable materials. And we can print buildings with any digital design our customers bring us. It's fast and cheap."[34]

Moreover, it may take the labors of dozens of tradespeople to build a single home—a factor that adds greatly to the cost. In contrast, WinSun was able to produce its 3D-printed homes with just a handful of workers, who fit the pieces of the houses together on-site in a matter of hours. "While a good chunk of the cost is raw building materials, another major source of cost and complications are the construction process and human construction workers,"[35] write Cornell University engineering professor Hod Lipson and technical writer Melba Kurman.

Printing Bricks

A process developed by CAD modelers at Cornell University in New York State in 2014 succeeded in fashioning bricks through additive manufacturing. Unlike the standard brick that has been used for centuries in the construction industry, these bricks require no mortar. Instead, the bricks include an interlocking feature that forms a weather-tight seal with no need for an adhesive between them.

Mortar is composed of cement, water, and crushed stone. It is laid across the tops, bottoms, and sides of bricks; when the mortar hardens, the seal becomes rock hard.

CAD modelers at Cornell call their bricks PolyBricks. They are made of ceramic material and shaped with grooves that enable them to lock together, forming a tight bond. Moreover, unlike conventional bricks, which are invariably manufactured in rectangular blocks, PolyBricks can be shaped to conform to the design of the building. If a building's walls are circular, PolyBricks can be printed in slight curves, enabling them to form a perfect circle when all are linked together. Jenny Sabin, a professor of architecture at Cornell who headed the project, explains:

> PolyBrick is the first mortarless, 3D printed wall assembly. It will allow for the production of ceramic wall assemblies that are robust and high strength due to the novel implementation of highly complex . . . design strategies that are also simply and economically produced. 3D printing allows us to build and design like nature does, where every part is different, but there is a coherence to the overall form.

Quoted in Daniel Aloi, "3-D Printing Helps Designers Build a Better Brick," *Cornell Chronicle*, July 28, 2014. http://news.cornell.edu.

Green Building

In the Dutch city of Amsterdam, architect Hedwig Heinsman heads a similar project—he hopes to 3D print a thirteen-room house along a canal in the city. But while WinSun uses mine refuse and other construction scraps as an additive in its printer, Heinsman is looking for an even greener alternative: He hopes to make use of an additive that contains 75 percent or more vegetable oil. Other components of the additive include wood scraps and plastic. "The building industry is one of the most polluting and inefficient industries out there," says Heinsman. "With 3D-printing, there is zero waste, reduced transportation costs, and everything can be melted down and recycled. This could revolutionise how we make our cities."[36]

The project commenced in 2014 as Heinsman's firm experimented with the composition of the additive. The project is making use of a printer known as the KamerMaker—Dutch for "room maker." The printer stands 20 feet (6 m) tall. It is large enough to print blocks that are 10 feet (3 m) high, which will be assembled into the home. By 2016 Heinsman was still experimenting with additives to determine which material would best suit his project.

Heinsman hopes to complete the project in 2017. In the meantime, he wonders whether a completely biodegradable additive can be employed to make temporary structures. After the structure is no longer used, it would decay on its own and eventually disappear. There would be no need to hire a demolition crew to tear down the structure and no need to find places to deposit the waste construction materials, such as old concrete and rusting metalwork. "One of my fantasies is printing in biodegradable materials for festivals," says Heinsman. "You could print an outrageous tent structure, then after a couple of years and few rain showers it disappears."[37]

D-Shape Building

Although visionaries such as Heinsman and Ma are spearheading projects to use 3D printing to create houses, their plans nevertheless call for making components of the homes, then piecing them together into completed structures. Other 3D-printing advocates believe it is possible to build an entire house, from the ground up, in one continuous printing process. By 2015 there were two methods under development for printing an entire house or similar building through 3D printing. These processes are known as D-Shape and Contour Crafting.

D-Shape was conceived by Dini, the civil engineer from Pisa, Italy. The additive for D-Shape printing—an SLS process—is sand. Under the D-Shape concept, to print a structure, the huge D-Shape device made of steel girders is trucked in pieces to the construction site, where it is assembled. Before printing begins, an architect, using CAD modeling software, has designed the home. On-site, a computer containing the plans is connected to the D-Shape printer. After the printer is assembled and the additive fed into the device, the printer operator presses Print on the machine, and the printing begins.

Unlike desktop printers or even most industrial models, the D-Shape printer employs numerous nozzles. Multiple nozzle heads speed up the printing process, given the enormity of the task undertaken by the printer. The nozzles are attached to robotic arms, which operate freely within the framework of the printer, going wherever the plans call for them to apply the additive.

Many hours later, the building has been printed, bottom to top, in one continuous process. Everything inside the house—the kitchen counter, stairways, doorways, walls, floors, and even channels for water pipes—would be printed in one process. Moreover, during the SLS process, the sand is fused together into a hard, marble-like substance, enabling the printer to create a sturdy structure. Says Monolite UK, "The process takes place in a non-stop work session, starting from the foundation level and ending on the top of the roof, including stairs, external and internal partition walls, concave and convex surfaces, bas-reliefs, columns, statues, wiring, cabling and piping cavities."[38]

Printing a Pool

By the time of this writing D-Shape printing was still very much in the experimental phase. The process had only been used to create a number of small structures such as gazebos for public parks. The current printer in use by Monolite UK measures about 30 feet in length by 30 feet in width (9 m by 9 m). Given the size of the typical house, which could span 1,600 square feet (149 sq m) and rise two floors above the ground, Monolite UK would need to develop a much larger printer to be able to print an entire house

A 3D printer constructs components for a planned thirteen-room house in Amsterdam, Netherlands. The project's architect, Hedwig Heinsman, hopes to make the project environmentally friendly by using an additive in the printing that is 75 percent vegetable oil.

in one continuous process. In the meantime, the company is using the D-Shape process much the same way that the projects headed by Heinsman and Ma are being printed: The D-Shape printer has been employed to create components for homes and other buildings that are then assembled into completed homes.

In 2015 Kushner, the New York City architect, announced the most ambitious plans to date to employ the D-Shape printer. He intends to partner with Monolite UK to create a luxury home in a suburb of New York City. The house, which Kushner will own, will cover 2,400 square feet (223 sq m) and include a swimming pool, pool house, and detached garage, all of which will also be made with the D-Shape printer. The components of the house, pool, and other structures will be printed on-site, then pieced together. The first step in the process will be to dismantle the D-Shape printer, which is in storage in Italy, and ship it to America to

Housing the Homeless

According to the US Department of Housing and Urban Development, about six hundred thousand Americans were homeless in 2014. Moreover, the United Nations estimates that worldwide, tens of millions of people have no permanent homes. 3D-printing advocates believe additive manufacturing could help end homelessness in America and elsewhere.

One advocacy group, the World's Advanced Saving Project (WASP), based in the Italian city of Massa Lombarda, believes 3D printing could help create homes for homeless people at little cost. Since the process would use clay dug out of the construction site, virtually the only cost of the homes would be the cost of transporting and operating the printer.

To print the homes, WASP has developed a 3D printer that stands 19 feet (5.9 m) tall. "We will print a mixture made of clay and sand," says Massimo Moretti, a spokesperson for WASP. "It takes weeks to print a real house, so we will print a smaller building. . . . But the print, the mixture and materials have been already tested and they're working."

WASP debuted its printing process at a conference of 3D-printing advocates in 2014 in Rome. WASP intends to raise money for its homelessness project by selling 3D-printed homes and buildings to individuals and businesses, then using the profits to print houses for homeless people.

Quoted in Eddie Krassenstein, "WASP Plans to Demonstrate New 6 Meter Tall 3D House Printer This Week," 3DPrint.com, September 30, 2014. http://3dprint.com.

commence the job, which is expected to take two years or more.

Moreover, Kushner hopes to use raw materials that are found on the site, such as sand and crushed stone, as the additive for the printer. He says, "The materials on the site will be used to form the pieces of the site, which reflects the very characteristics of the site, which stems from the materials found on the site. I think it's a perfect circle."[39]

Kushner says he is most intrigued about the notion of creating the swimming pool through 3D printing. The pool would, after all, have to be capable of withstanding water pressure. If a pool can be created through 3D printing, Kushner suggests that much more ambitious aquatic structures could also be created through additive manufacturing. He says, "If we can build a pool, then we can begin building reefs, and repair bridges, bulkheads and other underwater structures [where] there is a huge worldwide need."[40]

Contour Crafting

Although D-Shape printing has yet to create its first habitable structure, Dini and other proponents of D-Shape predict that as the technology advances, entire homes will eventually be built in one continuous process. Meanwhile, other experts are focusing on an alternative method for printing entire buildings: Contour Crafting. Developed by Behrokh Khoshnevis, a professor of industrial engineering at the University of Southern California (USC), Contour Crafting employs a mobile 3D printer that makes its way around the construction site either on free-roaming wheels or on rails that have been installed on the site. Essentially, the 3D printer is a robot. The CAD software that operates the program not only provides the robot with a design for the project but also directs its travel around the construction site, enabling the nozzle to discharge the additive according to the design. "You could set it up on a site to build one house or a whole row of houses,"[41] says Khoshnevis. The additive for the Contour Crafting process is composed of crushed concrete as well as an adhesive that binds the tiny concrete particles together. According to Khoshnevis, the Contour Crafting robot can build 1 square foot (0.09 sq m) of wall every twenty seconds. Moreover, Khoshnevis says, the Contour Crafting robot can go places that a D-Shape printer cannot go. Since the robot can be engineered to travel on rails, it can print very tall structures—such as skyscrapers—because it can climb rails that are erected vertically.

To pursue the technology, Khoshnevis has established the Contour Crafting program at USC's Viterbi School of Engineering. By 2016, though, the Contour Crafting process—as with D-Shape printing—had achieved just modest results, successfully printing structures that were no more than 7 feet (2.1 m) in height. Indeed, although Contour Crafting as well as D-Shape printing appear to hold great promise, proponents agree that creating entire houses and similar structures through the two processes are still years in the future. Reported the trade journal *Architectural*

A diver visits an artificial reef where marine life has flourished. Researchers believe that 3D printing could be used to manufacture such structures and also rebuild existing ones such as bridges and bulkheads.

Digest, "Though promising, 3D printing has yet to prove itself as a true force in the construction industry."[42]

Homeowners Designing Homes

Still, when the time arrives that processes such as D-Shape printing and Contour Crafting are employed routinely in the construction industry, Lipson and Kurman suggest that the next great advancement will be in CAD modeling. They suggest that professional CAD modelers may in the future no longer be needed to create the designs for homes. Rather, potential homeowners would be able to design the homes themselves by relying on easy-to-use software. The homeowners would tell their computers the type of features they want in their homes—the styles of the kitchens and bathrooms, for example. The software would then take over, producing designs that meet the preferences of the homeowners. Lipson and Kurman predict that CAD modelers could be freed from mundane chores such as designing kitchens and would instead be able to employ their talents for even bolder uses of the technology. Write Lipson and Kurman:

> Future humans will no longer spend time drafting and testing out possible design solutions. Instead, we will provide a Robotic Designer with a high-level concept of the design problem—its goals, its constraints, and its context. The human designer will define the parameters of the desired solution. Rather than being rendered obsolete by the new tools, future human designers, artists and architects will scale new creative heights.[43]

Of course, the technology has yet to advance to the stage that people can rely on their computers to design their homes for them. In the meantime, visionaries like Ma, Heinsman, Dini, and Khoshnevis know there is still much work to do in making the creation of a house produced in one continuous 3D printing session a reality.

Chapter 5

Launching 3D Printing into Space

There are more than two thousand satellites in earth orbit, performing a variety of chores for the United States and other nations as well as the private corporations that have been launching them since the 1950s. Some satellites help predict the weather by monitoring storms and other meteorological conditions in the atmosphere. Some satellites help drivers negotiate highways by providing information for Global Positioning Systems in their cars and trucks. Satellites launched by some countries are used for defense purposes, spying on enemies 100 miles (161 km) or more below.

Whether satellites are used to help guide vacationers on the highways or monitor the activities of terrorists, most satellites share a common trait: They are extremely expensive to build, launch, and maintain in orbit. Globalcom Satellite Communications, a Dallas, Texas, company that employs satellites to connect cell phone customers, estimates that it costs $290 million or more to build and launch a single satellite.

A major reason for the high cost of satellite technology is the method in which satellites are sent into space. They must be launched into orbit aboard a rocket—an expensive undertaking, given the cost of the vehicle, the fuel, and the launch facilities and personnel that must be devoted to the project. Moreover, the satellites must be built to withstand the tremendous forces of rocket flight as well as breaking away from Earth's gravitational pull. In addition, satellites are often limited in size and weight because they must fit into the noses of the rockets that boost them into orbit. And, certainly, adding to the cost is the possibility that the rocket could explode during or shortly after liftoff—a rare but not unknown occurrence over the years.

In coming years 3D printing is expected to have a major impact on the design, construction, and cost of launching satellites into earth orbit. Entrepreneurs are exploring the concept of equipping the International Space Station (ISS) with 3D printers capable of making the satellites in space. The satellites would then be launched as the station orbits Earth, meaning they would avoid the traumatic flight aloft aboard a rocket. "This is a fundamental shift for satellite production," says Andrew Rush, president of Made In Space, the Mountain View, California, company pursuing the technology. "In the near future, we envision that satellites will be manufactured quickly and to the customer's exact needs, without being overbuilt to survive launch or [having] to wait for the next launch."[44]

Printing a Rocket at Home

In the 1960s and 1970s, NASA sent humans to the moon aboard the Saturn V rocket. The huge rocket stood 363 feet (111 m) high. At liftoff, the rocket weighed 6.2 million pounds (2.8 million kg). The massive engine propelling the rocket was able to provide eighty-five times the power generated by the Hoover Dam.

In 2015 members of the University of California–San Diego's chapter of Students for the Exploration and Development of Space (SEDS) designed a miniature version of the Saturn V engine, which they 3D printed and successfully test fired in the Mojave Desert. The students' version of the Saturn V engine stands less than 1 foot tall (30 cm) and weighs 15 pounds (6.8 kg). The students believe they can eventually use the engine to launch a satellite into space.

If the SEDS chapter succeeds, it could pave the way for all those with a 3D printer to design their own rockets and satellites. Science writer Rod Pyle says the SEDS project reflects the thinking of the late physicist and science-fiction author Robert Forward, who predicted that one day ordinary people would find ways to access spaceflight. Pyle says, "Years ago, I attended a talk by a number of space luminaries, including Dr. Robert Forward. . . . The famed futurist said he expected we would grow rockets one day, just like we grow plants. At the time—this was in the 1990s—there was some grumbling and shuffling of feet in the audience. Today, while we might not be quite ready to grow a rocket, how about printing one?"

Rod Pyle, "Students Aim for Space with 3D-Printed Rocket Engine," Space.com, July 1, 2015. www.space.com.

3D Printing in Space

Manufacturing a satellite through the use of 3D printing—whether it is performed on Earth or in orbit—is a complicated undertaking. The printer would have to create the housing of the satellite as well as internal components such as the sophisticated electronics and optical features. In 2014 engineers at the National Aeronautics and Space Administration (NASA) Goddard Space Flight Center in Maryland commenced work on a 3D-printed camera and telescope intended for use aboard a satellite.

To build the camera and telescope, which is a single instrument, engineers used a laser to melt down a pile of metal powder. Next, they employed the SLS process to print the camera and telescope, layer by layer. According to Jason Budinoff, lead engineer on the project, the device was made on a 3D printer to show that additive manufacturing is a process that can be performed in space. Ordinarily, he says, a similar instrument may require the assembly of ten or more separate pieces. But NASA engineers combined the components into just four pieces, which were printed and then easily assembled. Given the tight confines of a spacecraft, the simplified manufacturing process would seem to be well suited for use in orbit. "I basically want to show that additive-machined instruments can fly," says Budinoff. "We will have mitigated the risk, and when future program managers ask, 'Can we use this technology?' we can say, 'Yes, we already have qualified it.'"[45]

Made In Space has even explored the possibility that the satellites could be 3D printed outside the cabin of the ISS, meaning the manufacturing would occur in space on an exterior platform affixed to the station. At the company's headquarters in Mountain View, engineers constructed a vacuum chamber to simulate the zero-atmosphere conditions in space. In 2015 Made In Space installed 3D printers in the vacuum chamber and printed tiny parts to test the concept of printing in the hostile environment of space. With the satellite

WORDS IN CONTEXT

microgravity
Gravity that is extremely weak; in an orbiting spacecraft, the microgravity is so weak that occupants and objects float freely.

A rocket carrying a satellite blasts off from Vandenberg Air Force Base in California. Scientists are pursuing the idea of equipping the International Space Station with 3D printers capable of producing satellites that would be launched directly from the space station itself, thus avoiding the cost, risks, and limitations associated with sending satellites into space aboard rockets launched from Earth.

actually printed outside the cabin, astronauts can easily release it into orbit once it is functional. "Soon, structures will be produced in space that are much larger than what could currently fit into a launch [vehicle], designed for microgravity rather than launch survivability,"[46] says Mike Snyder, chief engineer for Made In Space.

The notion that satellites could be 3D printed outside the ISS has been embraced by the National Academies of Sciences, Engineering, and Medicine, a Washington, DC–based independent research group that advises the federal government on science policy. In 2014 the National Academies released a report calling on NASA to support the expansion of 3D printing in space. In the report, the National Academies suggested that 3D printing in space could produce components more quickly than on Earth. Indeed, the report said, 3D printers operating on Earth are constrained by gravity: They must print one layer at a time, starting at the bottom and then slowly working their way to the top. But in a zero-gravity environment, the report said, such constraints are not present. Said the report:

> The lack of gravity and atmosphere presents possibilities for additive manufacturing in space not available to ground-based machines. The absence of gravity might permit a printer to work on the "bottom" and the "top" of an object at the same time. Imagine a printer for use in space that has multiple print heads and works on all six sides of an object resting in the space between the heads. Air jets or electrostatic attraction might be used to keep the growing object in place, or even to move it to the orientation most suitable for printing. For additive manufacturing in space . . . NASA has a unique opportunity to encourage innovative thinking about how to capitalize on the lack of gravity or the lack of atmosphere in space to better and more rapidly form objects that are similar to those made on Earth.[47]

Planning a Mission to Mars

The first steps toward making satellites as well as other devices in orbit occurred in September 2014 when Made In Space provided the ISS with a 3D printer designed to work in a zero-gravity environment. The printer was installed inside the ISS. To make the printer operational in zero gravity, Made In Space engineers

Printing a Pizza in Space

Bakers on Earth have used 3D printing to create customized chocolate candies. NASA believes 3D printing could also be used to feed astronauts for long-duration spaceflights.

Astronauts aboard the ISS receive food supplies when new missions arrive at the station. The food must be stored and refrigerated, which takes up a lot of the station's space as well as energy. NASA officials have acknowledged that it would be impractical to store and refrigerate the food it would take to sustain astronauts for flights to Mars that could last a year or more. In 2013 NASA asked the Systems and Materials Research Corporation (SMRC) of Austin, Texas, to study whether food could be 3D-printed in space.

Under the concept, foods would be processed on Earth, broken down into their basic components, and turned into powders. In flight the powders are used as the additive for the 3D printer.

In 2014 the SMRC unveiled the printer it designed for the project, demonstrating the device's capabilities by 3D printing a pizza. Said mechanical engineer Anjan Contractor:

> When astronauts press a button a little powder goes to a mixing chamber, water gets added, then it's pushed to the print heads. . . . As it's printing pizza it's also cooking, because the bed [onto which the dough is being layered] is hot. . . . And when it's finished the crust it starts on the tomato [sauce], and then after that it's the cheese. This is a complete process and after it finishes printing it can be eaten.

Quoted in Nate Lanxon, "3D-Printed Pizza and Tech 'Groundbreaking' for ISS," *Wired UK*, October 2, 2014. www .wired.co.uk.

designed the device to include an adhesive bed for the printer so that when the additive emerges from the nozzle, it sticks to the bed rather than flowing freely throughout the cabin.

The first 3D-printed object made in space was a wrench. To make the wrench, a Made In Space CAD modeler on the ground designed the tool, then e-mailed the design to the ISS. A crew member aboard the ISS printed the wrench, using the design. It took the Made In Space printer four hours to produce the wrench, which measures 4.5 inches (11.4 cm) in length and 1.3 inches (3.3 cm) in width.

NASA asked for a tool to be made because in planning for long-duration space flights, such as missions to Mars, astronauts may have to rely on 3D printing to make tools, spare parts, and other components since it would be impractical to supply the Mars-bound spacecraft with cargo once it leaves Earth's orbit. "3D printing offers considerable benefits in terms of spare parts," says Neil Leach, a professor of digital design at Harvard University in Cambridge, Massachusetts, as well as a consultant to NASA. "It makes more sense to be able to print spare parts on demand in space than to bring them on board, or have them delivered by a supply ship."[48]

Certainly, if astronauts can make a wrench on a 3D printer, they could make all manner of other objects—even habitats or other structures that could be erected on the surface of Mars. NASA and the European Space Agency (ESA), an agency supported by twenty-two European countries, are planning voyages to Mars. Such a voyage could take up to a year to achieve a landing on the planet, which is some 34 million miles (55 million km) distant from Earth. Given the time it would take to make the journey and the distance the mission would have to travel, the Mars-bound astronauts would be expected to spend several months if not years on the Martian surface.

Contour Crafting on Mars

Therefore, the astronauts would require habitats. To erect habitats for the crew members, as well as other buildings such as greenhouses, laboratories, landing pads, spacecraft hangars, and other storage facilities, NASA and the ESA are exploring the use of huge 3D printers—much as architects and construction companies are beginning to employ 3D printing to erect structures on Earth. Another group studying the concept is the Mars Foundation, a Massachusetts-based organization of scientists and engineers.

In fact, the two technologies that have received the most interest in being adapted for construction purposes on Mars are the

American astronaut Barry Wilmore displays a ratchet, one of several items that have been created by the first 3D printer installed on the International Space Station. The capability of producing tools and spare parts in space would eliminate the need to bring them on board initially or have them delivered on a supply ship.

same two technologies that are under development for construction purposes on Earth: D-Shape printing and Contour Crafting. In a statement, the Contour Crafting program at USC suggested the process could be ideal for creating habitats on Mars. Says the statement:

> Contour Crafting technology has the potential to build safe, reliable, and affordable . . . Martian structures, habitats, laboratories, and other facilities before the arrival of human beings. Contour Crafting construction systems are being developed that exploit resources [on Mars]. . . .
>
> The ability to fabricate extraterrestrial habitats, laboratories or manufacturing facilities is the key element for long-term human survival on . . . Mars. Our proposal develops an

automated . . . construction system that is viable, economical [and] practical.[49]

Leach cautions, though, that Contour Crafting as well as D-Shape printing must advance further on Earth before they could be considered for use on other planets. He says, "It is fair to say . . . that at present both suffer from insufficient prototyping in a terrestrial context. It makes little sense to send any robotic fabrication technology [into space] that has not been tried and tested fully on Earth, as maintenance would be a key issue. Both systems would need to be 100 percent reliable to be deployed in an extraterrestrial context."[50]

Martian Regolith

In fact, printing habitats on Mars would present some unique problems that engineers would have to tackle. For starters, the environment on the planet is nearly as unfriendly as the vacuum of space. The printer would have to function in an environment where the gravitational force is just 38 percent of that found on Earth. Also, the printer would have to operate in temperatures that, at the Martian equator, plummet to as much as -100°F (-73°C) at night. Also, the surface of Mars is constantly subjected to dust storms blown by winds that reach 68 miles per hour (109 kph).

However, officials of the Mars Foundation point out that although transporting and erecting the printers on Mars pose significant engineering challenges, the advantage of 3D printing on a distant planet is that the printer can make use of the raw materials found in the Martian soil. In other words, building materials such as concrete, steel, wood, and bricks would not have to be transported millions of miles to Mars. (Leach estimates that the cost of transporting a single brick into space could be as much as $2 million.) Instead, the rocky material found in the Martian soil can be used as the additive: fed into the printer, where it would be heated into molten form so that it emerges from the nozzle in whatever shape the CAD modeler has designed. "The key for living on Mars is to use the raw materials that are already there,"[51] says Bruce Mackenzie, founder and executive director of the

Mars Foundation. The Mars Foundation's initiative—which it has named the Mars Homestead Project—has made grants available to university scientists who are exploring methods for using native Martian minerals as the additive.

These minerals, known as regolith, are composed of sand and rocks found just below the loose soil on the planet's surface. The Martian regolith is believed to be rich in iron, meaning it could be heated into molten form, then used to print sturdy beams, walls, and other components for Mars-based habitats. Researchers are also exploring how the regolith can be used to make other construction materials, including cement, fiberglass, and plastics. "From the raw material already found on Mars, we can make plastics,"[52] suggests Mackenzie.

The Ice House

Other visionaries suggest, though, that regolith may not be the perfect additive for 3D-printed habitats on Mars. In 2015 NASA staged a competition for architects and other designers to propose concepts for a Mars habitat. The contest, known as the 3D-Printed Habitat Challenge Design Competition, drew thirty entries. The space agency awarded first prize in the competition to a group of eight architects who call themselves Team Space Exploration and Clouds Architecture Office. Team members called their proposal the Ice House because the structure resembles a large igloo. (The team members shared a $25,000 prize for the winning entry.)

As the name suggests, the additive for the Ice House would be ice, evidence of which has been found on Mars. Under the team's plan, the Ice House takes advantage of the planet's frigid temperatures by using an additive that would provide a sturdy habitat. Moreover, because it is made of frozen water, the Ice House would be translucent, letting in natural sunlight. The translucent nature of the Ice House saves energy because the inhabitants would not have to find a way to illuminate the habitat during daylight hours.

WORDS IN CONTEXT

radiation
Energy emitted by
the sun that travels
in waves or particles.

However, sunlight carries radiation that could prove harmful. On Earth, the sun's radiation can cause sunburns or, more severely, skin cancer. Even with those threats, most of the radiation is filtered out by the Earth's atmosphere. But the very thin Martian atmosphere would filter out far less radiation, posing a threat to the astronauts. Team members point out, though, that ice acts as a very capable filter for solar radiation and it would adequately protect the astronauts when they are in the habitat. Says a statement by the team:

The architecture of Ice House celebrates the presence of a human habitat as a beacon of light on the Martian surface. The design emerged from an imperative to bring light to the interior and to create visual connections to the landscape beyond, allowing the mind as well as the body to thrive. While scientists have experimented with what could potentially be synthetic replacements for sunlight, artificial substitutes do not hold nearly the same . . . ability to balance a crew's mental and physical health as does experiencing the sun's actual and unmediated daily cycles. The water ice counteracts the traditional danger of living above ground by serving as a radiation barrier, offsetting fears of solar exposure that have, until now, projected Martian architecture into a dark underworld—buried beneath a regolithic surface. . . .

By taking advantage of water-ice's ability to filter the sun's rays and protect against radiation, Ice House prioritizes a life above ground and celebrates the human presence on the planetary surface.[53]

Training for a Mars Mission

At this point, the Ice House as well as proposals to print habitats from Martian regolith are not much more than concepts. However, the Mars Foundation hopes to take creation of a Martian habitat

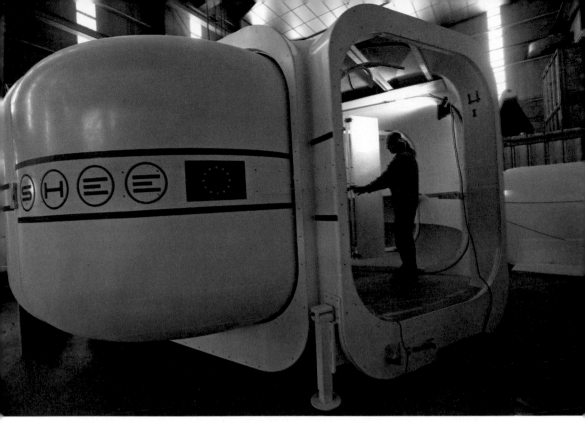

A technician works inside a habitat designed to support human operations in extreme environments. Scientists believe that 3D printing holds great promise for constructing such habitats to facilitate research on the planet Mars.

a step further by funding a 3D-printing research project at a facility known as HI-SEAS—the acronym stands for Hawaii Space Exploration Analog and Simulation. HI-SEAS is a compound located in a remote region on the island of Hawaii, near the Mauna Loa volcano. The compound, which is operated by the University of Hawaii and Cornell University in New York State, serves as a simulated Mars base; astronauts stationed at HI-SEAS train for a future Mars mission. According to the Mars Foundation, the soil at the compound is chemically similar to the soil found on Mars. Therefore, it provides ideal conditions to test the concept of converting regolith into an additive capable of large-scale printing projects—such as astronaut habitats, landing pads, and spacecraft hangars.

Although 3D printing holds great promise for providing habitats and other structures on Mars, spaceflight experts know there are many other hurdles to overcome before a mission to Mars is possible. In addition to finding a way to erect habitats on the planet, NASA and other space agencies and foundations have yet to figure out how to get there: Engineers must develop a spacecraft capable of making the journey. "We're setting expectations for something that is decades away,"[54] says Lori Garver, a former deputy NASA administrator. Indeed, most experts suggest that it will be at least the 2030s before astronauts set foot on Mars.

Despite the challenges that must be conquered before a trip to Mars is possible, people on Earth have envisioned missions to the planets for centuries. Scholars believed human flight to Mars and the other planets is within the reach of humankind long before the age of human space travel commenced in the 1960s. In 1657 the English architect and astronomer Christopher Wren said, "A time would come when Men should be able to stretch out their Eyes . . . they should see the Planets like our Earth."[55] And just as 3D printing is becoming a reality on Earth, in the future it is also possible that space travelers will be using the technology to make new satellites and tools, as well as new homes for themselves on Mars and other planets.

Source Notes

Introduction: The Potential of 3D Printing

1. Robert Sullivan, "Envisioning the Future of 3D Fashion: Welcome to the Virtual Dressing Room," *Vogue*, September 3, 2014. www.vogue.com.
2. Christopher Barnatt, *3D Printing: The Next Industrial Revolution*. Lexington, KY: ExplainingtheFuture, 2013, p. xi.
3. Quoted in Claire Barrett, "Everybody Could Have Their Body Scanned and Order Clothes That Fit Perfectly," *Dezeen*, April 24, 2013. www.dezeen.com.
4. Quoted in Sullivan, "Envisioning the Future of 3D Fashion."
5. Barnatt, *3D Printing*, pp. xi–xii.

Chapter 1: What Is 3D Printing?

6. Quoted in Rachel Ehrenberg, "The 3D Printing Revolution," *Science News*, March 9, 2013, p. 20.
7. Barnatt, *3D Printing*, p. 217.
8. US Department of Energy, "How 3D Printers Work," June 14, 2014. http://energy.gov.
9. Quoted in Stuart Nathan, "Ten Minutes with the Inventor of 3D Printing," *Engineer*, July 14, 2014. www.theengineer.co.uk.
10. Quoted in Nathan, "Ten Minutes with the Inventor of 3D Printing."
11. Quoted in David Mantey, "A Man & His Glue Gun," Manufacturing.net, June 14, 2012. www.manufacturing.net.
12. Quoted in Jessica Winter, "Everything That's Fit to Print," *Parade*, October 12, 2014, p. 9.
13. Quoted in Barnatt, *3D Printing*, p. 193.

Chapter 2: Opening a New Frontier in Transportation

14. James Derek Sapienza, "Can We Really 3D Print Cars and Car Parts?," Cheat Sheet, May 5, 2015. www.cheatsheet.com.

15. Jay Leno, "Jay Leno's 3D Printer Replaces Rusty Old Parts," *Popular Mechanics*, June 7, 2009. www.popularmechanics.com.

16. Quoted in Alexander George, "3-D Printed Car Is as Strong as Steel, Half the Weight, and Nearing Production," *Wired*, February 27, 2013. www.wired.com.

17. Quoted in Sarah Anderson Goehrke, "Local Motors to Begin Taking Pre-Orders Next Month for 3D Printed Cars," 3DPrint.com, September 18, 2015. http://3DPrint.com.

18. Quoted in Ehrenberg, "The 3-D Printing Revolution."

19. Quoted in Paulina Dao, "Robotboat: Transforming Ocean Research, One Boat at a Time," Planet OS, October 26, 2012. https://planetos.com.

20. Quoted in Dave Shively, "3D Kayak Engineering: Charlotte Paddler Creates the World's First 3D Printed Kayak," *Canoe & Kayak*, April 4, 2014. www.canoekayak.com.

21. Quoted in Parmy Olson, "Airbus Explores Building Planes with Giant 3D Printers," *Forbes*, July 11, 2012. www.forbes.com.

22. Quoted in Joseph Young, "3D Printed Aircraft Parts and Engines Could Lighten Aircrafts by 50 Percent," 3D Printing.com, June 7, 2015. http://3dprinting.com.

Chapter 3: Revolutionizing Medicine Through 3D Printing

23. Quoted in Roff Smith, "Just Press Print," *National Geographic*, December 2014, p. 126.

24. Quoted in Brandon Griggs, "The Next Frontier in 3D Printing: Human Organs," CNN, April 5, 2014. www.cnn.com.

25. Quoted in Alexander Trowbridge, "How 3D Printing Could Revolutionize Burn Treatment," CBS News, November 13, 2014. www.cbsnews.com.

26. Quoted in Erinn Hutkin, "3D Printing Takes Limb, Organ Replacement into New Dimension," *San Diego Union-Tribune*, June 16, 2015. www.sandiegouniontribune.com.

27. Quoted in Winter, "Everything That's Fit to Print," p. 13.

28. Quoted in Winter, "Everything That's Fit to Print," p. 13.

29. Quoted in Sarah Griffiths, "The Cheap Robotic Hand Set to Revolutionise Prosthetics: 3D-Printed Device Performs Advanced Tasks for a Fraction of the Cost," *Daily Mail* (London), September 8, 2015. www.dailymail.co.uk.
30. Quoted in *Telegraph* (London), "3D Printed Drugs Could Revolutionise Prescriptions," October 31, 2014. www.telegraph.co.uk.
31. Quoted in *Telegraph* (London), "3D Printed Drugs Could Revolutionise Prescriptions."

Chapter 4: From the Ground Up: Printing New Homes

32. Quoted in Tuan C. Nguyen, "Yes, That 3D-Printed Mansion Is Safe to Live In," *Washington Post*, February 5, 2015. www.washingtonpost.com.
33. Quoted in Nicola Davison, "3D-Printed Cities: Is This the Future?," *Guardian* (Manchester), February 26, 2015. www.theguardian.com.
34. Quoted in RT, "Giant Chinese 3D Printer Builds 10 Houses in Just 1 Day," April 27, 2014. www.rt.com.
35. Hod Lipson and Melba Kurman, *Fabricated: The New World of 3D Printing*. Indianapolis: Wiley, 2013, p. 189.
36. Quoted in Oliver Wainwright, "Work Begins on the World's First 3D-Printed House," *Guardian* (Manchester), March 28, 2014. www.theguardian.com.
37. Quoted in Wainwright, "Work Begins on the World's First 3D-Printed House."
38. Monolite UK, "The Technology," D-Shape, 2009. www.d-shape.com.
39. Quoted in Eddie Krassenstein, "Renderings and Details Unveiled for Extraordinary 3D Printed Home in New York," 3DPrint.com, April 23, 2015. http://3DPrint.com.
40. Quoted in Krassenstein, "Renderings and Details Unveiled for Extraordinary 3D Printed Home in New York."
41. Quoted in Brad Lemley, "The Whole House Machine," *Discover*, April 2005, p. 63.
42. Beau Peregoy, "The US Is Getting Its First 3-D-Printed House,"

Architectural Digest, June 9, 2015. www.architecturaldigest
.com.
43. Lipson and Kurman, *Fabricated*, p. 195.

Chapter 5: Launching 3D Printing into Space

44. Quoted in Mike Wall, "In-Space Satellite Construction May Be Coming Soon," Space.com, August 12, 2015. www.space
.com.
45. Quoted in Kelly Dickerson, "NASA Is Building the World's First 3D-Printed Space Cameras," Space.com, August 8, 2014. www.space.com.
46. Quoted in Wall, "In-Space Satellite Construction May Be Coming Soon."
47. Committee on Space-Based Additive Manufacturing, National Research Council of the National Academies, *3D Printing in Space*. Washington, DC: National Academies Press, 2014, pp. 2–3.
48. Neil Leach, *Space Architecture: The New Frontier for Design Research*. London: Wiley, 2015, p. 113.
49. Contour Crafting, "Space Colonies," 2014. www.contour
crafting.org.
50. Leach, *Space Architecture*, p. 113.
51. Quoted in Bahar Gholipour, "3D Printing on Mars Could Be Key for Martian Colony," Space.com, October 3, 2013. www
.space.com.
52. Quoted in Gholipour, "3D Printing on Mars Could Be Key for Martian Colony."
53. Quoted in Karissa Rosenfeld, "3D-Printed Ice Houses Win NASA's Mars Habitat Competition," *Huffington Post*, October 5, 2015. www.huffingtonpost.com.
54. Quoted in Joel Achenbach, "Could 'Martian' Happen? No Time Soon," *Philadelphia Inquirer*, October 4, 2015, p. A19.
55. Quoted in Carl Sagan, *Cosmos*. New York: Random House, 1980, p. 105.

For Further Research

Books

Christopher Barnatt, *3D Printing: The Next Industrial Revolution*. Lexington, KY: ExplainingtheFuture, 2014.

Samuel N. Bernier, Bertier Luyt, and Tatiana Reinhard, *Design for 3D Printing: Scanning, Creating, Editing, Remixing, and Making in Three Dimensions*. Sebastopol, CA: Maker Media, 2015.

Anna Kaziunas France, ed., *3D Printing: The Essential Guide to 3D Printers*. Sebastopol, CA: Maker Media, 2014.

Hod Lipson and Melba Kurman, *Fabricated: The New World of 3D Printing*. Indianapolis: Wiley, 2013.

Victoria Zukas and Jonas A. Zukas, *An Introduction to 3D Printing*. Sarasota, FL: First Edition Design, 2015.

Internet Sources

Claire Barrett, "Everybody Could Have Their Body Scanned and Order Clothes That Fit Perfectly," *Dezeen*, April 24, 2013. www.dezeen.com/2013/04/24/iris-van-herpen-interview.

Bahar Gholipour, "3D Printing on Mars Could Be Key for Martian Colony," Space.com, October 3, 2013. www.space.com/23059-3d-printing-mars-colony.html?li_source=LI&li_medium=more-from-space.

Eddie Krassenstein, "Renderings and Details Unveiled for Extraordinary 3D Printed Home in New York," 3DPrint.com, April 23, 2015. http://3DPrint.com/59753/d-shape-3d-printed-house-ny.

Karissa Rosenfeld, "3D-Printed Ice Houses Win NASA's Mars Habitat Competition," *Huffington Post*, October 5, 2015. www.huffingtonpost.com/entry/nasa-mars-habitat-competition_560ed558e4b076812701f204.

Dave Shively, "3D Kayak Engineering: Charlotte Paddler Creates the World's First 3D Printed Kayak," *Canoe & Kayak*, April 4, 2014. www.canoekayak.com/touring-kayaks/kayak-engineering /#hH46V1qAm7VOAsdj.97.

Websites

D-Shape (www.d-shape.com). Established by the British company Monolite UK, the website explains D-Shape printing and provides news and photographs of Monolite projects.

Enabling the Future (www.enablingthefuture.org). The website is maintained by the e-NABLE network, which uses volunteers to model and 3D-print prosthetic limbs. Stories about CAD modelers and recipients are available on the site.

Kor Ecologic (http://korecologic.com). The website provides updates and photographs on Kor Ecologic's plan to 3D print a car and drive it cross-country.

Mars Homestead Project (http://marshome.org). Maintained by the Mars Foundation, the website provides news, essays, and photographs on the group's Mars Homestead Project, which promotes creating habitats on Mars through 3D printing.

3DPrint.com (http://3dprint.com). The website tracks news in the 3D-printing and CAD-modeling industries. In addition to news stories, visitors can find forums in which readers discuss developments in 3D printing.

Index

Picture Credits

About the Author

Hal Marcovitz is a former newspaper reporter and columnist who lives in Chalfont, Pennsylvania. He has written nearly two hundred books for young readers. The author's daughter, Ashley Marcovitz, works as a CAD modeler in New York City.